MW01174345

WESTERN EDUCATIONAL ACTIVITIES LTD.
12006 - 111 Ave. Edmonton, Alberta T5G 0E6
Ph: (780) 413-7055   Fax: (780) 413-7056
GST # R105636187

BASIC / NOT BORING

READING

Grades 2-3

Inventive Exercises to Sharpen Skills and Raise Achievement

Series Concept & Development
by Imogene Forte & Marjorie Frank
Exercises by Marjorie Frank

Incentive Publications, Inc.
Nashville, Tennessee

About the cover:
Bound resist, or tie dye, is the most ancient known method of fabric surface design. The brilliance of the basic tie dye design on this cover reflects the possibilities that emerge from the mastery of basic skills.

Illustrated by Kathleen Bullock
Cover art by Mary Patricia Deprez, dba Tye Dye Mary®
Cover design by Marta Drayton, Joe Shibley, and W. Paul Nance
Edited by Anna Quinn

ISBN 0-86530-392-4

PRINTED IN THE UNITED STATES OF AMERICA

TABLE OF CONTENTS

Appendix

CELEBRATE BASIC LANGUAGE SKILLS

Basic does not mean boring! There is certainly nothing dull about clever circus clowns, adventuresome animals, and daring circus acts. It is so much fun to . . .

>   . . . solve the mystery of some stolen tacos
>   . . . unscramble mixed-up tickets and luggage
>   . . . play music for a snake
>   . . . order tasty pastries at a bakery in Paris
>   . . . wonder about strange disappearances in the Bermuda Triangle
>   . . . search for the Loch Ness Monster
>   . . . try to avoid the Abominable Snowman

These are just some of the topics young readers will explore as they celebrate basic reading skills. Each page of this book invites young learners to try a high-interest, visually appealing exercise that will sharpen one specific reading skill. This is not just an ordinary fill-in-the-blanks way to learn. These exercises are fun and surprising, and they make good use of thinking skills. Students will do the useful work of practicing reading skills while they enjoy following Aunt Frannie Frog on interesting adventures around the world.

The pages in this book can be used in many ways:
- to review or practice a skill with one student
- to sharpen the skill with a small or large group
- to begin a lesson on a particular skill
- to assess how well a student has mastered a skill

Each page has directions that are written simply. It is intended that an adult be available to help students read the information on the page, if help is needed. In most cases, the pages will best be used as a follow-up to a lesson that has already been taught. The pages are excellent tools for immediate reinforcement and sharpening of a skill.

As your students take on the challenges of these adventures with reading, they will grow! And as you watch them check off the basic language skills they've strengthened, you can celebrate with them.

The Skills Test

Use the skills test beginning on page 58 as a pretest and/or a post-test. This will help you check the students' mastery of reading comprehension and vocabulary skills and will prepare them for success on achievement tests.

SKILLS CHECKLIST
READING, GRADES 2-3

✔	SKILL	PAGE(S)
	Find the main idea of a passage	10, 11
	Find information on a map	12, 13, 23
	Read to find details	12, 13, 17, 18
	Follow written directions	14–16
	Read to find information	19–27
	Answer questions after reading a passage	19–27
	Match a story to a picture	19
	Find information on a chart	20
	Read titles to gain information	28
	Read to determine cause and effect	29, 30
	Identify sequence of events in a passage	31, 32
	Put words and sentences in proper sequence	31, 32
	Supply missing information for a passage	33
	Gain information from captions; match captions to pictures	34
	Determine author's purpose for writing a selection	35
	Make inferences about a passage	17, 18, 36, 37
	Make predictions after reading a passage	38, 39
	Give personal response to a passage	35, 38–43, 45
	Make an analysis of characters	43
	Distinguish fact from opinion in a passage	44
	Draw conclusions after reading a passage	45
	Identify exaggerations in a passage	46
	Complete similes	47
	Use context to decide word meaning	48, 49, 53
	Determine word meanings	48–56
	Complete analogies	54
	Recognize synonyms and antonyms	50, 55
	Identify words with multiple meanings	56
	Recognize and appreciate alliterative words and sentences	57

READING

Grades 2-3

Skills Exercises

Mail from Far-off Places

Aunt Frannie has friends and relatives all over the world. The mailman has just arrived with a lot of letters and packages for her.

As she reads her mail, Frannie starts to dream about faraway places. Soon she'll start looking at maps and visiting the travel agency!

Read each letter she has opened. Write the main idea of each letter.

June 1, A ship near Greenland

Dear Frannie,

We're on a ship off the coast of our country. This is the most amazing trip. You would not believe the icebergs in the water around us. They are huge! They are mountains! Some tower 200 feet above our ship! It seems as if we are floating among gigantic castles. Their shapes are strange and wonderful and different, but mostly, we are just shocked by their awesome size!

Wish you were here!

Love, Opi and Omi

The main idea is _____

_____

_____

1.

The world is so small...

Miss Gloria Hollywood, CA U.S.A.

Greta Fogg Amsterdam Holland

Gracia Rosa Madrid, Spain

Frannie Frog 1450 Lilypad Swampville U.S.A.

Omi & Opi Greenland

Frannie Frog 1450 Lilypad Lane Swampville, NC, U.S.A.

June 14, China

Dear Frannie,

I think you'll like this picture of a giant panda. Today, I'm off hiking with a group that's searching for the panda. We know these bears sleep in trees during the day, so we are looking in the bamboo forests. So far, we have had no luck. We have looked for 3 days. I am so anxious to see at least one! Most of all, I want to see some panda cubs. Wish me luck!

Love, Gonzo

The main idea is _____

_____

2.

3.

Madrid, Spain
June 25

Dear Aunt Frannie,

You wanted to hear about the bullfight, didn't you? I'm not sure you will like what you hear! It was so dreadful. I was frightened most of the time. It seemed so cruel to stab the bull and make him angry. The bull-fighter had a lot of skill, but he was badly injured. I closed my eyes most of the time, because it was so awful. The crowd cheered. They loved it! I won't ever watch one again.

Love, Roxy

The main idea is

_____

_____

_____

4. Australia, June 19

Dear Frannie,

Here's a surprise for you—a boomerang from Australia. It will not be easy to use. I thought I could just toss it, and it would come right back to me. Wow! Was I ever wrong! It was so hard to learn. I had to practice for about a year, but it is so much fun! Maybe you'll learn faster than I did. Have fun!

Cousin Rudy

The main idea is _____

_____

Name _____

It's a Big World out There

Aunt Frannie has caught the travel bug. Her Travel Wish List is growing longer. Today, she has started putting pins on a world map to mark some places she would like to visit.

Read the Wish List and the map to answer the questions on the next page (page 13).

Travel Wish List

Grand Canyon
Sahara Desert
Bermuda Triangle
Alaska & Canada
African Jungle
Everglades Swamp
Loch Ness
The Great Pyramids
Paris, France
Great Wall of China
Hollywood
Music City–Nashville
Angel Falls
Australia's Outback
Amazon Rain Forest
Submarine Ride
India & Italy
Antarctica
Siberia
The Himalayas

North America

South America

Flippity-doo-da! Pack my bags! I'm going on a worldwide trip!

Basic Skills/Reading 2-3

It's a Big World out There, cont.

EUROPE

ASIA

AFRICA

AUSTRALIA

I'm going shopping for some new duds!

1. How many pins has she put on Africa? _____
2. How many pins are on South America? _____
3. How many pins are in the ocean? _____
4. What desert would she like to see? _____
5. What does she want to see in Scotland? _____
6. What ride would she like to take? _____
7. What does she want to see in China? _____
8. What swamp does she want to visit? _____

ANTARCTICA

Name _____

Use with page 12.

(13)

Read for Details • Read a Map

Off to the Travel Shop

There's a good travel shop at the mall where Aunt Frannie went to buy things for her trip. Read about her shopping trip below. Use a marker or crayon to draw the path she took to the travel shop.

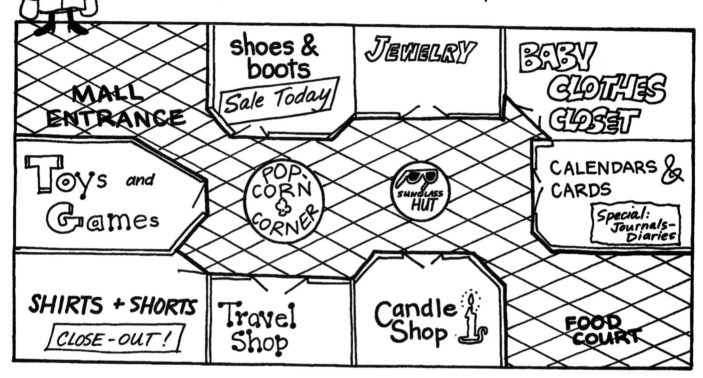

1. First, Frannie bought hiking boots at the shoe store.

2. Next, she got a new calendar to keep track of her travels.

3. Frannie bought two pairs of good sunglasses at the Sunglass Hut.

4. She stopped for a big box of popcorn.

5. Frannie went to the jewelry store for a waterproof diving watch.

6. Next, she shopped for Bermuda shorts at the Shirts & Shorts Shop.

7. She bought toys to take to nieces and nephews in China.

8. She got hungry for some pizza, so she headed to the food court.

9. Finally, she bought luggage and other supplies at the travel shop.

Name _____

Read to Follow Directions

Basic Skills/Reading 2-3

Where Are the Backpacks?

Oops! The travel shop is not ready for customers yet. Some merchandise needs to be put on the shelves. Follow the directions to finish putting out the supplies.

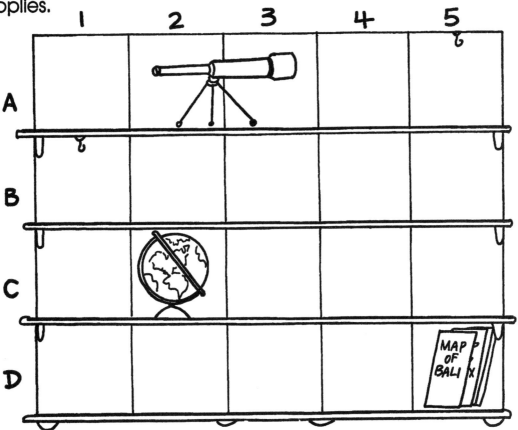

Draw these things on the grid:

1. Draw a backpack hanging in A, 5 and B, 5.
2. Draw a travel book on India in C, 1.
3. Draw a travel book on Alaska in A, 1.
4. Draw a travel book about Mexico in D, 1.
5. Draw a travel clock in D, 4.
6. Draw a travel pillow in D, 2.
7. Draw some bug spray in C, 4.
8. Draw some sunscreen lotion in B, 3.

Name _____

Read to Follow Directions

Baggage Confusion

There's trouble on the baggage carousel. Tags and labels have fallen off suitcases everywhere. Follow the directions to get things back to normal.

1. Draw a sticker for Brazil on Maria's luggage.

2. Write Percy Penguin's name on the tag of the bag with the Australia sticker.

3. The bag with the China sticker needs Lu Sing's name on the tag.

4. Draw a sticker for Hawaii on Chester's luggage.

5. Write Frannie Frog's name on the bag with the Swampville sticker.

6. The bag with the Nashville sticker needs a tag for Dolly Dimples.

Name _____

Read to Follow Directions

Ticket Mix-up

Oh, no! Frannie has just discovered that she has the wrong ticket! She needs a ticket to Mexico. Straighten out this ticket mix-up. Read the information on the tickets to finish the sentences and questions below.

1. The yacht ticket belongs to Jenny Jinx. Write her name on it.

2. Waldo is traveling to Texas. How will he get there? _____

3. The plane ticket to Singapore belongs to _____.

4. Will Zeke travel to Greenland by plane? _____

5. Find Mrs. Smuggs' ticket. Where is she going? _____

6. Where is Frank Frog headed? _____

7. Bart is going to the Super Bowl. How is he traveling? by _____

8. Find Frannie's ticket. How is she traveling to Mexico? by _____

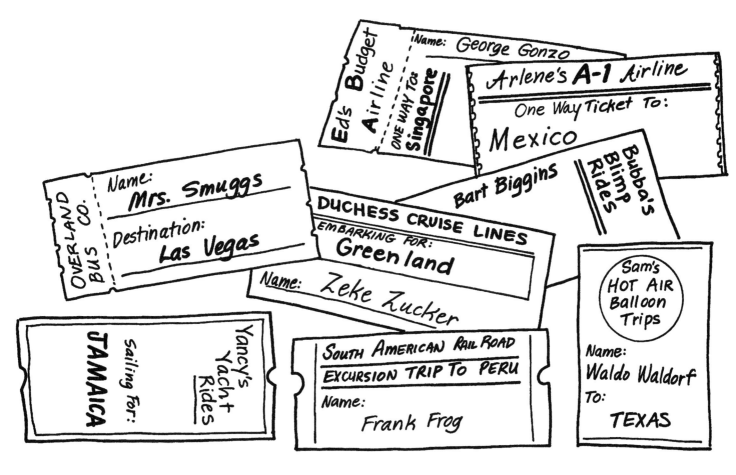

Name _____

Read for Details • Inference

The Great Taco Mystery

There are 500 tortillas missing from Cousin Pepito's Taco Stand in the little Mexican town of Las Truchas! They were stolen some time between 6:00 and 8:30 A.M. Boot-like footprints were found at the stand. Read the clues to help him solve the crime before Aunt Frannie arrives for lunch.

Clue # 1
Santos works at the Las Truchas Motel from midnight to 9:00 A.M. He has greasy fingers. He says it is from maple sugar candy.

Clue # 2
Candita has drips of something greasy on her skirt and pieces of lettuce stuck in her teeth. She left home at 8:00 A.M. It takes 40 minutes to drive into Las Truchas.

Clue # 3
Pedro says he was sleeping until 10:00 A.M. His boots have crunchy crumbs stuck to them. He has a large sack in his truck. It has crunchy crumbs in it.

Where are those tacos?

Who do you think stole the tacos?

_____

Why do you think so? _____

_____

_____

_____

What do you think he or she did with the tacos? _____

_____

_____

Name _____

Cruising through the Rain Forest

Cousin Felix has convinced Frannie to join him on an Amazon River cruise through the rain forest.

Look at the picture. Then read the story. Circle words or phrases in the story that do not match the picture.

Cruising along with the Alligators

Oh, what a lovely, rainy day! Frannie has her camera out to take pictures from the jungle cruise boat. She is just arriving in Amazonia to stay at the Raindrop Resort. Her boat will stop near Bill's Boat Rentals where there are four boats for rent. Five other little boats are floating nearby on the river, and a lazy gorilla is enjoying a float on the cool water. "Look at those alligators snoozing in the hammocks," she says to Cousin Felix. She is excited to see the little café, because she's very hungry from her trip. She thinks she will join the two black panthers at the café table. Frannie is happy to get off the boat and enjoy a cool drink. "I love this place!" she exclaimed. "It's too bad there are no umbrellas at the café to protect us from the hot sun."

Name _____

Read for Information

Record Setters

"I want to visit the coldest spot, the longest cave, the hottest desert, and the tallest waterfall in the world!"

Read the chart to help Frannie find information about some of these places.

WORLD RECORD SETTERS

Place	Location	Length	Cost
Longest Cave	Mammoth Cave Kentucky	4 days	$1200
Largest Desert	Sahara Desert North Africa	1 week	$3500
Biggest Island	Greenland	2 days	$800
Highest Waterfall	Angel Falls Venezuela	3 days	$1000
Tallest Building	Petronas Towers Malaysia	3 days	$1000
Coldest Town	Norlisk Russia	9 days	$4200

1. Which trip costs the most? _____

2. How long is the trip to the Sahara Desert? _____

3. What is the biggest island? _____

4. In what country is the coldest town? _____

5. What is the tallest building? _____

6. How long is the trip to the highest waterfall? _____

7. How much does it cost to get to the longest cave? _____

8. Which trip takes the longest? _____

Name _____

The Big Drop

Finally! After a long, muddy bus ride from Brazil to Venezuela, Frannie can set her eyes on something she has dreamed of seeing all her life—the world's tallest waterfall!

A Lucky Discovery

In 1933, an American named James Angel went to Venezuela. He landed his small plane to look for gold, but his plane would not take off again. He had to walk a long way back to a city. On the way, he was lucky enough to discover the world's tallest waterfall. It was named after him. It's called Angel Falls. He never did get his plane back. It wasn't rescued until 37 years later! This was after he had died.

World's TOP 10 Waterfalls

Angel Falls . . . Venezuela
Tugela . . . South Africa
Utigard . . . Norway
Mongefossen . . . Norway
Yosemite . . . United States
Ostre Mardola . . . Norway
Tyssestrengane . . . Norway
Cuquenan . . . Venezuela
Sutherland . . . New Zealand
Kjellfossen . . . Norway

3212 feet

ANGEL FALLS BUS LINE

1. How many of the world's top ten highest falls are in Norway? _____

2. Which country has two of the top ten waterfalls? _____

3. The tallest waterfall in the U.S. is 2425 feet high. What is it? _____

4. Which waterfall is in South Africa? _____

5. Which waterfall is in New Zealand? _____

6. What was James Angel looking for in Venezuela? _____

7. In which year was his plane found? (Use your math skills!) _____

Name _____

Read for Information

Special Permission Required

It's good that Cousin Maxie is a scientist. Otherwise Frannie might not be able to visit the Galapagos Islands. Visitors are allowed only with special permission. Take some bug spray, Frannie! The mosquitoes are huge!

My family has lived on this island....

..for a 1000 years!

The Galapagos Islands

They are called "the end of the world." The nine Galapagos Islands are located in the Pacific Ocean several hundred miles west of Ecuador. The Islands are covered with many volcanic craters from volcanoes that blew their tops. What is so special about these islands anyway? When scientists first came here, they found plants and animals that were different from those anywhere else in the world. The islands are filled with giant land iguanas, interesting birds, and giant turtles. Sea iguanas and sea lions fill the waters around the island. Very few people live on the islands, which are owned by Ecuador. They've been turned into a national park and wildlife sanctuary.

1. The Galapagos Islands are in the _____ Ocean.

2. Who owns the islands? _____

3. What is unusual about the animals there? _____
_____

4. Name an animal Frannie will see on the islands. _____

5. How many people live on the islands? _____

6. What two kinds of iguanas can be found? _____

7. What caused the craters? _____

Name _____

Basic Skills/Reading

Not on a Yacht!

Is there a stowaway on board the *Princess Frog* yacht? Mysterious things keep happening on Frannie's cruise. Use the map of the yacht and the clues to find the mysterious passenger. *(A stowaway is a passenger that did not pay and had to sneak on board!)*

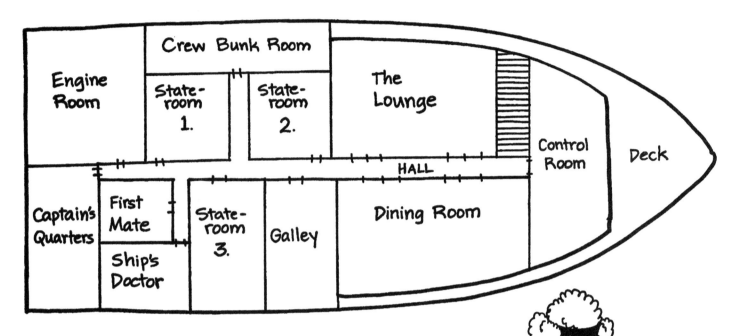

1. The visitor is not in the dining room.

2. The visitor is very small.

3. The visitor is not in the doctor's room.

4. The visitor loves to nibble scraps of food.

5. The visitor is not in the first mate's quarters.

6. The visitor has a tail.

7. The visitor is in a room that is next to stateroom 3.

8. Where is the visitor? _____

9. What or whom do you think the visitor is? _____

_____

Name _____

Read for Information • Read a Map

Streaks across the Sky

What's that flaming streak that Frannie is watching from the deck of the ship? Read the passage below to find out. Then answer the questions.

What's That Flash in the Sky?

A flaming streak flashes across the sky!
Now it's gone! Did you see it? What was it?

On many nights, blazing trails of light can be seen across the dark sky. These are really small chunks of matter from outer space burning up in Earth's atmosphere. Before the chunks enter Earth's atmosphere, they are called meteoroids. As soon as they enter the atmosphere, they become meteors.

Most meteors burn up before they reach Earth's surface. Some meteors are so large that they fall all the way to Earth before they burn up entirely. If one does hit Earth, it becomes a meteorite. Thousands of meteoroids enter Earth's atmosphere every year, but only about 500 reach Earth.

1. What are the chunks called after they enter the atmosphere? _____

2. What are they called before they enter the atmosphere? _____

3. What are they called when they hit Earth? _____

4. What happens to most meteors? _____

5. About how many meteorites reach Earth each year? _____

6. What word is used to describe the trails of light? _____

7. Where do meteoroids come from? _____

8. How many meteoroids enter the atmosphere each year? _____

Name _____

Strange Events at Sea

It's brave of Frannie to sail this way across the Atlantic Ocean. She's headed right through the Bermuda Triangle!

Finish the puzzle with information from the paragraph about the Bermuda Triangle.

DISAPPEARED!

The Bermuda Triangle is an area in the Atlantic Ocean shaped like a triangle. It is found between the Southern United States coast, the island of Bermuda, and a group of islands called the Greater Antilles. For over 100 years, people have reported strange happenings in this place. It is said that over 70 ships and airplanes have disappeared in this area, but no one has ever found any wrecked boats or planes or any other proof that anything has happened!

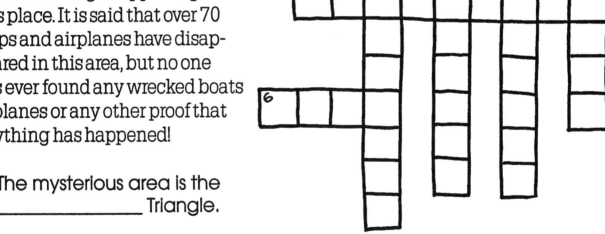

1. The mysterious area is the _____ Triangle.

2. There is no _____ of any of the rumors.

3. People say that things _____ in the Bermuda Triangle.

4. How many ships and planes are missing? _____

5. What is supposed to have disappeared? _____

6. How many wrecked planes or ships have been found? _____

Name _____

A Stop at the Pastry Shop

Ahhh, Paris! There's nothing like a morning visit to the pastry shop on a Paris corner. Gaze at the Eiffel Tower while you enjoy a whipped cream cake (or two)!

Menu

francs

chocolate éclair — 15

caramel cream — 10

strawberry crepe — 15

cheese pastry — 14

whipped cream cake — 25

French bread — 13

cinnamon bun — 10

apple tart — 14

lemon custard — 11

mocha crepe — 15

Wheeeee

Oui.

Answer these questions about what's on today's menu.

1. How much would two cinnamon buns cost?

   _____

2. What is the most expensive item on the menu? _____

3. What two kinds of crepes could Frannie try?

   _____

   and _____

4. Which is more expensive, two éclairs or three lemon custards?

   _____

5. What is more expensive than a crepe?

   _____

6. What costs the same as a cinnamon bun?

   _____

7. How much would an apple tart and a cheese pastry cost? _____

8. Which item from the menu do you think Frannie will like best?

   _____

Name _____

Basic Skills/Reading 2-3

Keeping Watch for Nessie

Great-Uncle Fergus McFrog recites a poem for Aunt Frannie while they're out sightseeing on the famous Loch Ness.

The sailors say it's down there,
Hidden, lurking, deep,
Waiting in murky waters,
Waiting, but not asleep.

The Loch Ness Monster they call it—
Thirty feet long, at least.
Many say they have seen it,
But no one can catch the beast.

No ship is safe from danger,
From the coils of this monstrous snake.
No ship can escape when it rises
From the bottom of the Scottish lake.

Wait in the foggy darkness.
Watch from the ship's front rail.
Look in the black, cold waters.
Look! Do you see that tail?

Beautiful, Fergus! What an imagination.

1. Write three words used to describe the waters of the lake.

_____ _____ _____

2. How long do they say the monster is? _____

3. What word in the first verse means "waiting"? _____

4. Where does the monster live? _____

5. Where is this lake? _____

6. What does the word "foggy" describe? _____

7. Do you think the Loch Ness Monster is real? _____

Name _____

A Midnight Visitor to the Castle

Someone is sneaking into the library of Zamalot Castle deep in a forest in Germany. Who could it be?

The visitor notices that the names of the authors are missing from the books.

Read each book title, and decide which author matches the book. The clues are hidden in the authors' names. Write the number of the book next to the author's name.

① Dreadful Dragons by ?

② How To Build A Moat by ?

③ The Ballad Of The Princess And The Frog by ?

④ Cooking in the Castle by ?

⑤ THE BEST ARMOR CATALOGUE by ?

⑥ The Laws Of The Kingdom by ?

⑦ DUNGEON POETRY by ?

⑧ The World Is FLAT! BY ?

⑨ SONGS FROM THE TOWER BY ?

⑩ The Collected Jokes Of A CLOWN by ?

Authors

_____ Dewey U. Swim   _____ O. Watta Suit

_____ Nerv S. Knight   _____ Queen Ima Ruler

_____ Sing A. Long   _____ Chef Barbie Q.

_____ A. Jester   _____ Ben Caught

_____ Professor Pancake   _____ Great-Great-Aunt Florence Frog

Name _____

What Caused the Blisters?

Third cousin Gerta von Frog is taking Frannie on a stroll through the famous tulip gardens of Holland. Unfortunately, Frannie has terrible blisters on her feet. What caused the blisters?

Here are some things that happened while Frannie was in Holland.

Find the causes and effects that match, and you will find out about the blisters! Color each pair the same color to show what caused each event below. Use a different color for each of the six pairs.

CAUSES

Frannie bought some new wooden shoes.
The hotel ran out of apples.
Another tourist sat on Frannie's camera.
The tulip gardens are in full bloom.
The bus to Amsterdam had a flat tire.
Frannie ate four pounds of Dutch chocolate.

EFFECTS

Frannie arrived late at her hotel.	Thousands of visitors have come to Holland.
The chef baked berry pies.	Frannie had huge blisters on her toes.
Frannie spent two days in bed sick.	Frannie had no pictures of Holland.

Name _____

Headlines from Italy

A.
Italia Press

TRAVELERS STRANDED

1. The airport was fogged in.
2. People had to stay in hotels.
3. Some suitcases were lost.

B.
La Roma Times

TOWER FALLS ON TOURIST

1. An earthquake shook the Tower of Pisa.
2. The tourist sneezed.
3. A tourist stood by the tower.

C.
Florence Daily

ART TREASURES STOLEN

1. The paintings were fakes.
2. A thief was caught.
3. No one locked the museum door.

To catch up on the news, Frannie stopped by a newsstand in the city of Pisa, Italy. Did she find some interesting headlines?

Read the headline on each newspaper. Then write the number of the statement that shows what probably caused that headline to be written.

A. _____
B. _____
C. _____
D. _____
E. _____
F. _____

D.
Venice Daily

GONDOLA CAPSIZES

1. A tourist rocked the boat.
2. Many people got wet.
3. A sea monster made huge waves.

E.
Venice News

OPERA SINGER HITS HIGHEST NOTE

1. A bee stung her as she sang.
2. She wore a new costume.
3. She had a sore throat.

F.
Pisa Gazette

SPAGHETTI-EATER HOSPITALIZED

1. A new restaurant opened.
2. He ate too much in an eating contest.
3. The hospital was hit by a tornado.

Pardon me Senora,...

Do you have the Swampville Gazette ?

Sorry!

Can you tell me where to get a pizza ?

News-stand

Name _____

Such Nonsense!

While Frannie was visiting Limerick, Ireland, she had such fun reading all the limericks written by Edward Lear. He was a famous writer of limericks. He even wrote a book of limericks called *The Book of Nonsense.*

Three of these limericks are a bit mixed-up! Unscramble them.

Number the lines in the correct order. Then enjoy reading them.

There was a Young Lady whose chin
Resembled the point of a pin;
So she had it made sharp
And purchased a harp,
And played several tunes with her chin.

B.

____Who was horribly bored by a Bee;
____He replied, "Yes, it does!
____When they said, "Does it buzz?"
____It's a regular brute of a Bee."
____There was an Old Man in a tree,

A.

____When the door squeezed her flat,
____Who casually sat in a doorway;
____There was a Young Lady of Norway
____She exclaimed, "What of that?"
____This courageous Young Lady of Norway.

C.

____Have all built their nests in my beard."
____There was an Old Man with a beard,
____Two Owls and a Hen,
____Four Larks and a Wren,
____Who said, "It is just as I feared!

Name _____

Scrambled Phone Conversations

When Frannie called Cousin Toad, there was a bad phone connection. Toad got everything all mixed-up. Then he called Uncle Hopper to tell him about Frannie's call, and he got things more mixed-up!

For both phone calls, number the sentences in the right order.

Frannie called Cousin Toad back home in Swampville.

- [ ] **Guess what? I'm in Tanzania, Africa!**
- [ ] **Good-bye, Cousin!**
- [ ] **I went on a safari.**
- [ ] **I took lots of pictures of the mountain.**
- [ ] **Hello! I want to speak to Toad.**
- [ ] **I'll send you some shots.**
- [ ] **The safari went near Mt. Kilimanjaro.**

Cousin Toad called Uncle Hopper about Frannie's phone call.

- [ ] **First she went to Dan and Zia's.**
- [ ] **Have you heard about Aunt Frannie?**
- [ ] **She wore a sari there!**
- [ ] **Hello, Uncle Hopper.**
- [ ] **Good-bye, Uncle!**
- [ ] **Then she rode a killer banjaro.**
- [ ] **And she's sending the jackpot tomorrow.**

Name _____

Trouble in the Jungle

Oh, no! It looks as if Frannie has stumbled across a big problem on her visit to the African jungle. Read the story, and fill in the parts that are missing with a word or phrase. Make sure your story matches the picture.

She was having a nice tour of _____ , listening to the chattering of the birds and monkeys. Then she heard _____ . When she peeked through the tall plants to see what was happening, she saw that _____ over a fire. Then she realized that those frogs were her nephews! She _____ , screaming and waving her arms. They had to stop! She never thought a minute about her own safety. She just knew that she had to _____ . Well, wasn't Frannie surprised when she learned what was really going on? Her nephews were not really in any _____ . They were just playing a part in a jungle movie. They were pretending to get cooked. They were even getting paid for it!

Name _____

Supply Missing Information

Missing Captions

A photo album is a good way to remember a trip. Frannie has forgotten to put the captions with her pictures from Africa. Help her do that before she forgets what happened on this trip. Draw a line from each caption to the matching picture. She forgot to write one caption. Write it for her and match it to the right picture.

We visited the Hippo Mud Spa.

I took a quick dip in Lake Makat.

I flew over Ngorongoro Crater

I camped in the fig trees near the Lerai Forest.

I liked Ed, my elephant guide.

Basic Skills/Reading 2-3

Curious about Mummies

What a shock to come face-to-face with a mummy! Aunt Frannie got a big surprise when she visited the pyramids in Egypt. She learned that one of her distant relatives actually lived there a long, long time ago!

HOW TO MAKE A MUMMY

People are very curious about mummies. Did you ever wonder how they are made?

Mummies are bodies that have been preserved. Long ago, Egyptians made mummies of their rich kings (called pharaohs) and rulers. First, the body was preserved with spices. After about 70 days, the body was wrapped in cloth. Usually the mummy was put into a wooden case or wrapped in cloth made stiff with glue. The Egyptians wrote and painted things about the person's life on the outside of the case. Often they painted a mask on the end of the case. Sometimes people made mummies of animals that had special meaning, especially cats.

It's my great-great-great-great-great-great-great Uncle Pharaoh!

Why do you think the author wrote this ?

_____

_____

_____

Name _____

Author's Purpose

Who's Going to Tahiti?

Fog has closed down the airport. Not one plane can leave for hours! Aunt Frannie is keeping herself busy by trying to guess where the other passengers are going. Read the clues to find out who is going to Tahiti.

Write the name of the place where each passenger is going above his or her head.

1. The passenger between the lizard and the porcupine is going to Spain.

2. The prickliest passenger is going to Germany.

3. The smallest traveler is going to Peru.

4. The elephant is definitely not going to Tahiti.

5. The passenger with the baby is going to Australia.

6. The passenger with the longest nose is going to Omaha.

7. Aunt Frannie is not going to Tahiti.

8. Who is going to Tahiti? _____

Name _____

Inference

Basic Skills/Reading 2-3

Who Owns the Helicopter?

One of these vehicles is waiting to take Aunt Frannie to the train station in Siberia. The other vehicles are waiting for other passengers. Read the clues to figure out which one is for Frannie. While you're looking for that, figure out who owns the helicopter!

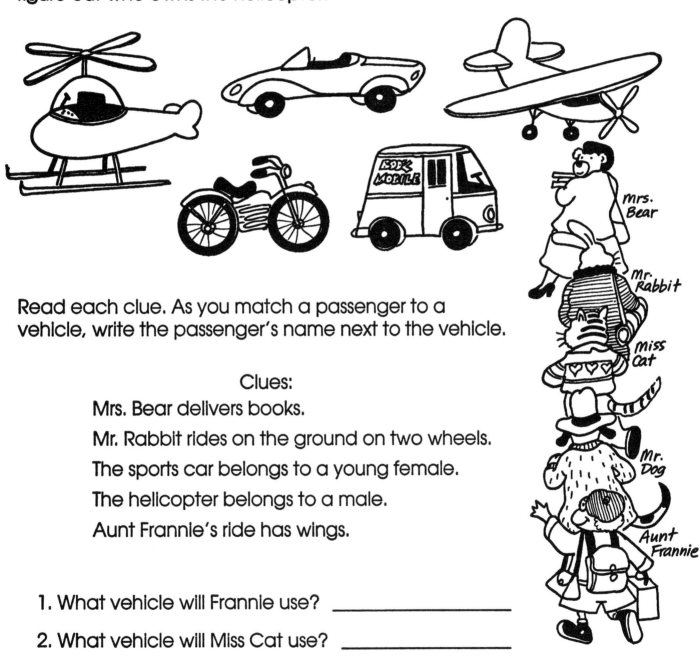

Read each clue. As you match a passenger to a vehicle, write the passenger's name next to the vehicle.

Clues:

Mrs. Bear delivers books.

Mr. Rabbit rides on the ground on two wheels.

The sports car belongs to a young female.

The helicopter belongs to a male.

Aunt Frannie's ride has wings.

1. What vehicle will Frannie use? _____

2. What vehicle will Miss Cat use? _____

3. Who owns the helicopter? _____

Name _____

Copyright ©1998 by INCENTIVE PUBLICATIONS, INC., Nashville, TN.
Basic Skills/Reading 2-3

Inference

The Night Train

On a snowy night, passengers are making a long trip across Siberia in northern Russia. Frannie has a feeling that this will be an unusual trip. Read about Frannie's strange train ride.

The night is very stormy as the train speeds across the open fields of Siberia. Snow is piling up on the railroad tracks. Sometimes the train moves very slowly through the snow. Twice the train has had to stop to wait for snow to be shoveled from the tracks.

The passengers have settled down for a long ride. Aunt Frannie notices a mysterious passenger walking down the aisle. He has a very lumpy overcoat. Frannie has a feeling that there is something very strange about him. He is moving slowly and looking over his shoulder often. He keeps his hands in his pockets.

Suddenly, the train screeches to a halt with a loud "THUD!" The lights go out. Passengers scream!

Tell what you think will have happened when the lights come back on.

_____

_____

_____

Name _____

Dear Diary

The Himalayas are the highest mountains in the world. Aunt Frannie cannot wait to get up into those mountains and climb!

Read some of the things she has written in her diary. Write her diary entry for the day of the climb. What did she write that day?

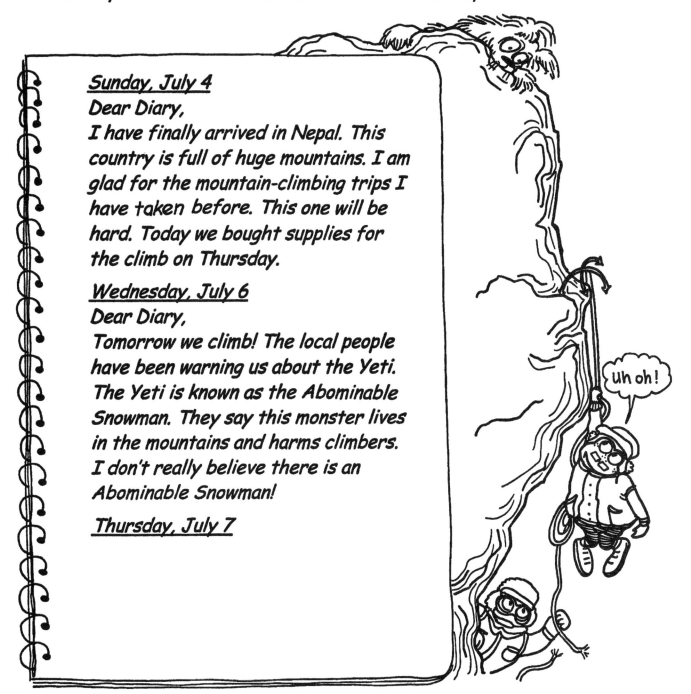

Sunday, July 4
Dear Diary,
I have finally arrived in Nepal. This country is full of huge mountains. I am glad for the mountain-climbing trips I have taken before. This one will be hard. Today we bought supplies for the climb on Thursday.

Wednesday, July 6
Dear Diary,
Tomorrow we climb! The local people have been warning us about the Yeti. The Yeti is known as the Abominable Snowman. They say this monster lives in the mountains and harms climbers. I don't really believe there is an Abominable Snowman!

Thursday, July 7

uh oh!

Name _____

Music for a Snake

In India, Frannie gets a chance to join a snake charmer as he tries to get the snake to dance. What a huge and amazing animal! Frannie never thought she would be playing music for a snake!

Read the shape poem about the snake. Then tell what you think about the poem.

Slowly, slowly, out of the basket, the silky snake slides and slithers. Its smooth skin shines in the sparkling sunlight. Slowly, slowly, the snake sways to the soft sounds of the music.

What do you think about the snake poem?

_____

_____

_____

Write some words that helped you imagine the snake. _____

_____

_____

Name _____

What's Your Fortune?

How many relatives does Frannie have in China, anyway? She's having dinner tonight with all of them. They are all looking forward to the end of the dinner, because they all love to eat fortune cookies.

Read the fortunes from the cookies. Then choose fortunes for Frannie and yourself.

1. This is Not a good week to travel.

2. It is better to try and fail, than to do nothing.

3. Beware of high places!

4. You will learn something important from a friend.

5. Do not wear socks for seven days.

6. A dragon will tell you a secret soon.

7. A surprise will come to you in a faraway place.

8. Tomorrow you will have a wish come true.

1. Choose a fortune for Frannie. #_____. Tell why you think she should have that fortune.

_____

2. Which fortune would you like to get? #_____. Why? _____

_____

_____

Name _____

Would You Go There?

Signs on post:
- Nose-Freezing Temperatures Ahead!
- SOUTH POLE 20 miles (Don't Go There)
- ICE ABYSS 10 PACES

Scientific Outpost

Not many people travel to Antarctica. Would you? Frannie couldn't stay away. She has always wanted to see this cold, far-off continent. Now that her good friend Penelope Penguin is working in Antarctica, she has a good excuse to visit. Read some facts about Antarctica, and decide if it's a good place for Frannie to be.

CHILLY ANTARCTICA

- It is covered with a sheet of ice.
- The ice sheet is thousands of feet thick.
- It is the coldest place on the Earth.
- No people live there permanently.
- It is too cold for plants to live.
- It is the windiest place on Earth.
- The cold is so extreme that it is dangerous.
- The average temperature is 70° below zero.
- The lowest temperature is 128° below zero.

Should Frannie stay here a long time? Would you visit this place? Tell what you think!

_____

_____

_____

_____

_____

_____

_____

_____

_____

Name _____

Personal Response

Copyright ©1998 by Incentive Publications, Inc., Nashville, TN.
Basic Skills/Reading

Relatives on the Reef

The Great Barrier Reef off the coast of Australia is the largest coral reef in the world—1250 miles long! It is a great place for diving and snorkeling. Read the snorkelers' thoughts below. How would you describe their feelings?

Write the number of the snorkeler that matches each word.

____ helpful   ____ frightened   ____ selfish

____ excited   ____ bored   ____ grumpy

Name _____

Character Analysis

Opinions from Hawaii

These postcards are ready to send to relatives and friends back in the USA. Frannie has written facts and opinions about her visit to Hawaii. Can you tell which are which?

Read each postcard. Find the sentences or phrases that show Frannie's opinions. Circle them in red. Circle facts in blue.

1. Dear Frankie,
Hawaii is wonderful. You should have seen me at my hula lesson! It lasted one hour. I was pretty silly-looking, but I sure did like the grass skirt! The food here is wonderful. They serve meals all day. See you in September.
Love, Aunt Fran

Frankie Frog
1111 Hwy 66
Ashland, OR
97520

2. Dear Mandy,
My hotel is a bit dumpy. I think it is also overpriced. It costs $100 a day because it is on the beach. The hotel staff is not friendly, and there are too many mosquitoes! The beach is the best part!
Love, Aunt Frannie

Mandy Froglegs
4100 Mud Lane
Swampville, NC
01007

3. Dear Sammy,
Today I took a helicopter tour over the volcanoes of Hawaii. There are many active volcanoes in Hawaii. It is amazing! The tour lasted 3 hours. The helicopter pilot was from Singapore. I thought the view was beautiful.
Love, Aunt Frannie

Sammy Leaper
20 River Rd
Green River, CA
94221

Name _____

First to Fly

The Frog family has a history of setting records in the air. Some of Frannie's relatives have been the first frogs to take flights in balloons. On her hot air balloon ride, she's telling her nephew Felix a little bit about the family's past adventures.

Read the labels on the balloons. Then answer the questions.

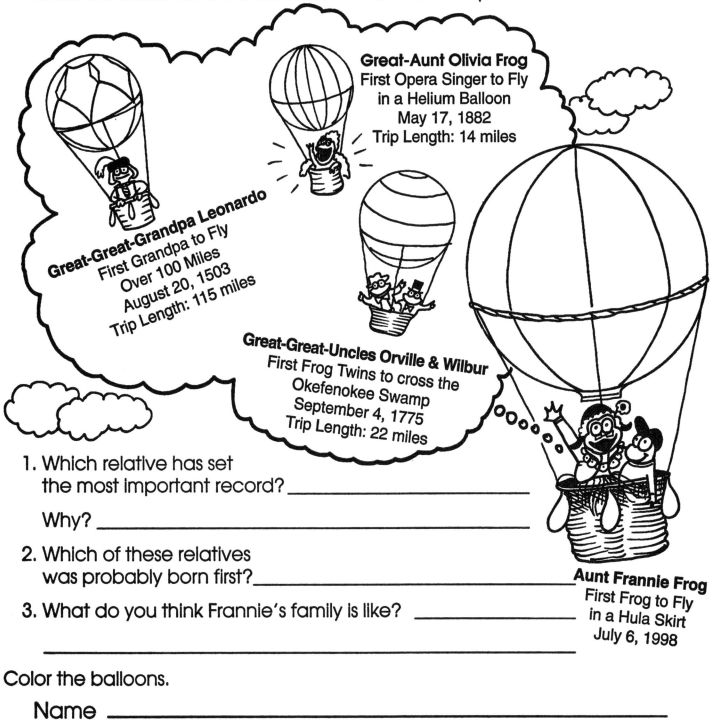

Great-Aunt Olivia Frog
First Opera Singer to Fly
in a Helium Balloon
May 17, 1882
Trip Length: 14 miles

Great-Great-Grandpa Leonardo
First Grandpa to Fly
Over 100 Miles
August 20, 1503
Trip Length: 115 miles

Great-Great-Uncles Orville & Wilbur
First Frog Twins to cross the
Okefenokee Swamp
September 4, 1775
Trip Length: 22 miles

Aunt Frannie Frog
First Frog to Fly
in a Hula Skirt
July 6, 1998

1. Which relative has set
   the most important record? _____

   Why? _____

2. Which of these relatives
   was probably born first? _____

3. What do you think Frannie's family is like? _____
   _____

Color the balloons.

Name _____

Draw Conclusions

Tall Tales from the Arctic

The plane was not supposed to land here! Frannie was on her way to Alaska, but the plane got a bit lost and ended up much farther north.

She can't believe how cold it is! Read the tall tale she wrote later about her stop in the Arctic. Look for her exaggerations.

A Tall, Tall Tale

It's a wonder I survived one day in the arctic. It was so cold that my nose turned into an icicle the minute I stepped off the plane. My fingers became long ice cubes and broke right off. As I walked away from the plane, my shadow froze to the side of the plane and couldn't follow me. When I sneezed, the drops of mist turned to snowflakes and dropped to the ground. The plane landed very near to a farm where a farmer was milking cows in a barn. It was so cold that the milk came out of the cow as ice cream. I tried to say "hello" to the farmer, but the words froze before they reached him. I picked up a stick to help me walk through the snow back to the plane. Later, when it got warm inside the plane, the stick thawed out and crawled away. It was snake! I was sure glad to leave that cold place!

An **exaggeration** is telling more about something than is actually true.

1. Draw a circle around every statement in the tale that is an exaggeration.

2. Write one exaggeration of your own about the cold.

_____

_____

_____

_____

_____

Name _____

A Great Fishing Story

Fishing is a good topic for great stories. Often people stretch the truth a bit when they talk about the fish they caught. A fishing story is best when the writer uses phrases that compare things to each other. Finish each of these similes that Frannie started. You can use the ideas here or create your own! (A **simile** is a comparison between two things that are not alike. It uses the words *like* or *as*.)

Writing Starters

- an apartment building
- running a marathon
- a fighting tiger
- climbing a mountain
- a speeding train
- crushed icebergs
- wrestling an alligator
- a mad dog

- fireworks
- a bull
- a tiger
- iron
- a blimp
- lightning
- a tunnel
- black coffee
- a school bus
- a beachball
- the moon

- a whale
- a racing stallion

The fish that got away was as big as _____

The first fish I caught was as fat as_____

Catching that 100-pound fish was like_____

The river was rushing as fast as _____

The night was as dark as _____

The water was cold like _____

The moon was as bright as _____

The fish fought like _____

That fish was tough like _____

Name _____

Copyright ©1998 by Incentive Publications, Inc., Nashville, TN.
Basic Skills/Reading 2-3

Similes

Safety on the Slopes

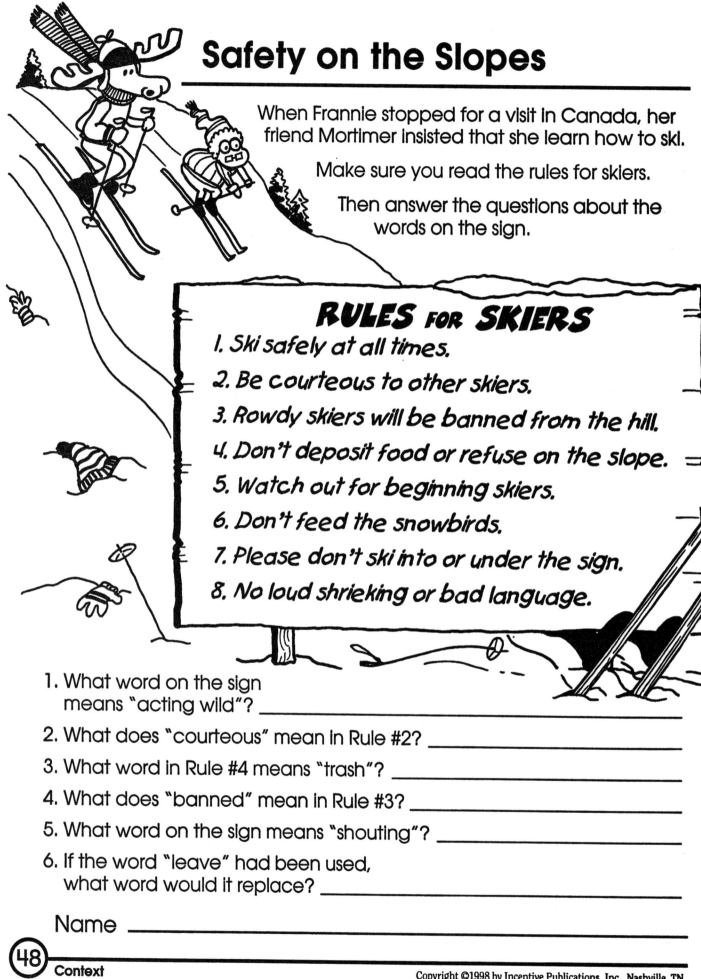

When Frannie stopped for a visit in Canada, her friend Mortimer insisted that she learn how to ski.

Make sure you read the rules for skiers.

Then answer the questions about the words on the sign.

RULES FOR SKIERS

1. Ski safely at all times.
2. Be courteous to other skiers.
3. Rowdy skiers will be banned from the hill.
4. Don't deposit food or refuse on the slope.
5. Watch out for beginning skiers.
6. Don't feed the snowbirds.
7. Please don't ski into or under the sign.
8. No loud shrieking or bad language.

1. What word on the sign means "acting wild"? _____

2. What does "courteous" mean in Rule #2? _____

3. What word in Rule #4 means "trash"? _____

4. What does "banned" mean in Rule #3? _____

5. What word on the sign means "shouting"? _____

6. If the word "leave" had been used, what word would it replace? _____

Name _____

Letter from the Lodge

Frannie has a little extra time for writing letters. Read the letter she's writing to her friend Abigail. Then answer the questions about her letter.

Mt. Whistler Ski Lodge
Whistler, Canada

Dear Abigail,
I should not have listened to that stubborn Mortimer! He insisted that I must learn to ski. Well, I made a good effort, but you know how clumsy I am! The trees were too massive and too close together. The skis were too slick. Now, look at me! What a monstrous mess I am! Here I am, all droopy and lonely in the lodge. My leg is wrapped up with ghostly white fabric. To walk, I have to use two sticks that look like wishbones. I am sorry to repeat myself, but I will. I should not have listened to Mortimer!
Love,
Your ailing friend, Frannie

1. Which word means "strongly stated"? _____

2. Which word means "slippery"? _____

3. Which words mean "huge"? _____

4. How does she describe her mood? _____

5. How does she describe her crutches? _____

6. What word means "sick" or "not doing well"? _____

7. What words are used to describe
   the fabric around her leg? _____

Name _____

Context

A Famous Sidewalk

Frannie couldn't wait to get to Hollywood to visit her movie star friend, Gloria Frogarella.

Now Gloria has taken Frannie to see the famous Hollywood Walkway of the Stars.

Look at the words in each star. If the star contains a pair of synonyms, color the star gold.

wild savage

rapid speedy

difficult simple

prevent stop

simple easy

rough smooth

destroy ruin

never often

weary tired

ugly beautiful

frighten scare

steal rob

Name _____

Where Would You Find It?

Do you know what a gorge is?

Where would you find one?

Frannie is visiting the largest gorge in the world—the Grand Canyon. It is a deep valley cut through stone by the rushing Colorado River. It is 277 miles long!

Circle the answer that tells where you would find each of these.

Where would you find . . .

1. . . . a glacier?
   a. in the Arctic
   b. in the desert
   c. in your freezer

2. . . . a baboon?
   a. on an iceberg
   b. in the jungle
   c. in your shoe

3. . . . a synonym?
   a. in a story
   b. in your soup
   c. on a spider

4. . . . a carousel?
   a. on a map
   b. at a fair
   c. in a bathroom

5. . . . a zucchini?
   a. in a shoe store
   b. in a post office
   c. in a garden

6. . . . a peninsula?
   a. on a map
   b. in your lunch
   c. at a hospital

7. . . . an omelette?
   a. in a swimming pool
   b. on a plate
   c. in a jewelry store

8. . . . a hearth?
   a. near a fireplace
   b. in a sandwich
   c. in a sink

9. . . . a sum?
   a. in a car engine
   b. in a math problem
   c. in a birdcage

10. . . . a vessel?
    a. in a tool box
    b. in your body
    c. in a milkshake

Name _____

Word Meaning

What Would You Do with It?

What would you do with a lasso? At a Dude Ranch in Texas, Frannie and her twin sister Freeda are learning what to do with a lasso.

Circle the answers that tell what you would do with these other things!

What would you do with . . .

1. . . . a spatula?
   a. put it in the bank
   b. flip a pancake with it
   c. eat it

2. . . . a blimp?
   a. ride in it
   b. spend it
   c. swim in it

3. . . . a treasure?
   a. swallow it
   b. take a bath in it
   c. hide it

4. . . . a trophy?
   a. put it on a shelf
   b. cook it
   c. spread it on toast

5. . . . a forecast?
   a. put it in a toolbox
   b. listen to it
   c. dance with it

6. . . . a casserole?
   a. bake it
   b. bury it
   c. study it

7. . . . a vitamin?
   a. copy it
   b. rearrange it
   c. swallow it

8. . . . marmalade?
   a. rent it
   b. spread it on toast
   c. write it down

9. . . . an antique?
   a. give it a bath
   b. treasure it
   c. munch on it

Name _____

Word Meaning

Basic Skills/Reading 2-3

Welcome to Music City, USA!

Cousin Twila Crocker wrote a song about Nashville. Frannie is lucky enough to get there just in time to hear Twila perform at the Grand Ole Opry!

Read Twila's song.

Then answer the questions about some of her words.

Grab your gal, and grab your man.
Have some fun with a band.
The Country Music Hall of Fame
Has more stars than you can name!

The Grand Ole Opry–you must see
When you come to Tennessee.
Come on in, reserve a seat.
The music makes you tap your feet!

Join right in! Grab your guitar!
You might get to be a star!
You could try to write a song.
The whole gang will sing along.

Take a seat and sit a while.
Country music makes you smile.
Listen all you want–it's free!
Why don't you stay in Tennessee?

Write words from the song to complete these problems.

Write a word that means . . .

1. take hold of _____

2. great _____

3. save _____

4. group _____

5. entire _____

Write the opposite for each word . . .

6. less _____

7. city _____

8. give _____

9. leave _____

10. frown _____

Name _____

Word Meaning

Bumper Stickers in New York

What interesting bumper stickers Frannie is seeing in New York City! Each pair of bumper stickers compares one set of things to another. All the bumpers today have half of a bumper sticker. Each pair of bumper stickers compares one set of things to another. Draw lines to match the two halves.

Example:

Stop is to go . . . as up is to down.

Hungry is to eating

Lawyer is to courtroom

Fingers are to typing

BUS

Grumpy is to happy

Monkeys is to monkey

Cold is to freezing

as feet are to climbing.

as nervous is to relaxed.

as mice is to mouse.

TAXI

XYZ 123

as doctor is to hospital.

as warm is to hot.

as tired is to sleeping.

Name _____

A Strange Weather Report

Wilbur is the new weather reporter for a big TV station in Minnesota. Tonight he is so nervous that he is getting the report mixed-up. He keeps saying the opposite of what he means to say!

Circle all the wrong words in Wilbur's report. Then write the correct word (the opposite) on one of the lines.

TELE-PROMPTER

Bad evening, folks!

Welcome to the station that gives you the worst, most incomplete weather report in town. I came in late today and worked easily to get none of the latest facts about the weather. I'll tell you about the weather today, and then sooner, I won't give you the forecast for yesterday. Today, it was warm and sunny. It was cold and sunny at midnight, with a temperature of 85°. Tomorrow it will be hot again all night until evening. Then the weather will warm, with temperatures dropping below 50°.

Well, that's it for now, folks. Enjoy this terrible weather today. Please don't tune in again tomorrow. We'll have less weather for you!

_____

_____

_____

_____

_____

_____

_____

_____

_____

_____

_____

_____

_____

_____

WEATHERFROG
WILBUR
W-FROG Ch. 50
NEWS AT 11:00

Name _____

Antonyms

Welcome Back!

All the friends and neighbors in Swampville are happy to have Frannie back home. When they say "welcome back," they are using one meaning of the word **back**. It has other meanings, too. Maybe Frannie has a tired **back,** or maybe she needs to **back** her car out of the driveway!

Each sentence shows one meaning of the word in bold type.
Write a sentence that shows a different meaning of the word.

1. This brick is **light** to carry.

   _____

2. I need a **saw** to cut this board.

   _____

3. I ate a **quarter** of your pizza.

   _____

4. I **can** do this hard math.

   _____

5. What do you **mean** by that?

   _____

6. I got a good part in the **play.**

   _____

7. Don't peel **bark** off that tree!

   _____

8. **Duck,** or you'll hit your head!

   _____

Name _____

What a Way to Wander the World!

"What a way to wander the world!"
Frannie says to her friends.

"I've seen slithering snakes, creepy castles, and dazzling disappearances!"

Frannie is using sentences with **alliteration.**

She puts words together that begin with the same consonant sounds.

Read the silly sentences in her journal. In each sentence, circle the sounds that are the same.

Frannie's Silly Sentences

1. Sid's sister searched seven Siberian cities for six Saturdays.

2. Fat frogs find fun at the Fudge Factory in Frankfort.

3. Chew chunky chocolates and tasty truffles in a Paris café.

4. Polly picked a pyramid as the place to plant her petunias.

5. I sniffed and sneezed for seventeen seconds.

6. You can't catch a cough or a cougar in Canada.

7. Which way do you wish to walk in Wichita?

8. You'll never need knickers in Nashville!

9. Texas Todd climbed ten tall towers.

10. Homer Hamster hurried home to Hollywood.

Name _____

Alliteration

Reading Skills Test

Read the following poem, and then answer the questions.

Ernie stepped in quicksand
Even though the sign was there.
He walked right into the middle
Though the sign told him, "Beware!"

The sand was filled with water,
Which turned it into muck
All wet and thick and gooey,
Poor Ernie was out of luck!

His feet sank in up to the knees
He tried to run on through.
He grabbed and pulled and hollered,
But the quicksand was like glue.

We all went out to find him.
Poor Ernie was up to his ears.
We threw him a rope and dragged
   him out,
And he's lived for years and years!

1. A good title for this poem would be
   a. Ernie's Walk
   b. Foolish Ernie
   c. All About Sand

2. Where did Ernie step into the
   quicksand?
   a. the edge
   b. the river bottom
   c. the middle

3. How many people went to
   look for Ernie?
   a. No one
   b. One person
   c. Many people

4. What word in stanza #3
   is a synonym for **yelled?**

   _____

5. What did the sign tell Ernie?

   _____

6. What did Ernie do after he sank
   into the quicksand?

   _____

7. Write three words the poem used
   to describe the quicksand.

   _____

   _____

   _____

8. What kind of a person do you think
   Ernie was?

   _____

Name _____

**Look at each pair of sentences. Write C in front of the cause.
Write E in front of the effect.**

9. ____ The ship was tossed around wildly.
   ____ A terrible hurricane crossed the ocean.

10. ____ The airport was surrounded by heavy fog.
    ____ No airplanes could take off yesterday.

11. ____ The volcano erupted again last week.
    ____ The sky is filled with ash.

12. ____ We explored the island on motorbikes.
    ____ No cars are allowed on the island.

13. This limerick is mixed-up!
    Number the lines in the correct order.
    ____ So why was he giggling
    ____ A certain young man from France
    ____ And shaking and wiggling?
    ____ It's because he was covered with ants!
    ____ Was always too bashful to dance.

Read the paragraph, and answer the questions.

Frannie started up the helicopter motor. She shouted to Felix, "Are you ready?" "Yes!" he hollered. "Let's take off!" And off they went, flying over the bridge. Then Felix had an idea. "Let's try flying under the bridge!" he shouted.

14. What do you think will happen next?

_____

_____

15. Find a pair of synonyms in the story. _____ , _____

16. Find a pair of opposites. _____ , _____

17. What did Frannie start? _____

Name _____

Reading Skills Test

Finish the sentences.

18. **Wet** is to **rain forest** as **dry** is to _____ .

19. **Morning** is to **evening** as **day** is to _____ .

20. **Submarine** is to **airplane** as _____ is to **above.**

21. **Child** is to **children** as _____ is to **geese.**

Read the passage, and answer the questions.

Yum

A long time ago in the jungle, a big, fierce lion caught a tiny mouse for a snack. Just as the lion was about to gobble up the mouse, the mouse cried, "Oh please! Please! Don't eat me! If you let me go, I promise to come back and help you some day!" Now the lion thought that was pretty funny that such a tiny thing could help him, the king of the jungle! While he was laughing, the mouse escaped and ran away.

Many days later, the big, powerful lion, was caught in a tricky trap set by some lion hunters. The mouse was far away, but he heard the lion's painful roar. He ran quickly through the jungle and found the trapped lion. "Here I am to help you!" cried the mouse. This time, the lion did not laugh. He needed all the help he could get! The tiny mouse gnawed the ropes off the lion. In no time at all, the lion was loose again. From that day on, the lion and the mouse were best friends.

22. How did the mouse escape from the lion? _____

23. When did this story take place? _____

24. What word describes the trap? _____

25. What word describes the lion's roar? _____

26. What word means the same as **mighty?** _____

27. What title would you give to this? _____

28. This story is a fable. A fable teaches a lesson. What lesson does this teach?

_____

_____

Name _____

Read the passage, and answer the questions.

   In 1980, Mt. St. Helens, in Washington, erupted three times in two months. The first blast was 500 times as powerful as an atom bomb. The volcano caused 60 deaths. It caused three billion dollars in damage.

   A volcano is an opening in the surface of the Earth. Gases and melted rock erupt through the opening. There are over 500 active volcanoes in the world today. Some volcanoes are slow and quiet, but many are very violent. The big explosions do a lot of damage.

   Here is an example of the harm a volcano can do. A volcano on an island in Indonesia killed 2000 people in 1883. The next day, the mountain collapsed. This killed 3000 more people. The collapse of the mountain caused a huge tidal wave in the ocean. That wave crashed onto other countries and killed another 31,000 people.

29. When did Mt. St. Helens erupt? _____

30. How many active volcanoes are there in the world today? _____

31. Is it true that all volcanoes erupt violently? _____

32. What was the cost of the eruption at Mt. St. Helens?

    _____ people and _____ dollars

33. How many deaths were caused by the tidal wave? _____

34. What is the main idea of this passage? _____

    _____

    _____

35. What do you think the author's purpose was in writing this passage?

    _____

    _____

    _____

Name _____

Answer Key

Basic Skills/Reading 2-3

page 21
1. 5
2. Venezuela
3. Yosemite Falls
4. Tugela Falls
5. Sutherland Falls
6. gold
7. 1970

page 22
1. Pacific
2. Ecuador
3. Some of the animals are not found anywhere else in the world.
4. Answers will vary.
5. very few
6. giant land iguanas and sea iguanas
7. volcanoes

page 23
8. Galley
9. Answers will vary—perhaps a mouse or rat

page 24
1. meteors
2. meteoroids
3. meteorites
4. They burn up.
5. 500
6. blazing
7. outer space
8. thousands

page 25
1. Bermuda
2. proof
3. disappear
4. seventy
5. planes
6. none

page 26
1. 20 francs
2. whipped cream cake
3. strawberry and mocha

4. 3 lemon custards
5. whipped cream cake
6. caramel cream
7. 28 francs
8. Answers will vary.

page 27
1. murky, black, cold
2. 30 feet
3. lurking
4. Loch Ness
5. Scotland
6. darkness
7. Answers will vary.

page 28
1. Nerv S. Knight
2. Dewey U. Swim
3. Great-Great-Aunt Florence Frog
4. Chef Barbie Q.
5. O. Watta Suit
6. Queen Ima Ruler
7. Ben Caught
8. Professor Pancake
9. Sing A. Long
10. A. Jester

page 29
C—Frannie brought new wooden shoes.
E— Frannie had huge blisters on her toes.
C—The hotel ran out of apples.
E—The chef baked berry pies.
C—Another tourist sat on Frannie's camera.
E—Frannie had no pictures of Holland.

C—The tulip gardens are in full bloom.
E—Thousands of visitors have come to Holland.
C—The bus to Amsterdam had a flat tire.
E—Frannie arrived late at her hotel.
C—Frannie ate four pounds of Dutch chocolate.
E—Frannie spent two days in bed sick.

page 30
A. 1   D. 1
B. 1   E. 1
C. 3   F. 2

page 31
A. 3, 2, 1, 4, 5
B. 2, 4, 3, 5, 1
C. 5, 1, 3, 4, 2
Also accept 5, 1, 4, 3, 2

page 32
A. 2, 7, 3, 5, 1, 6, 4
B. 3, 2, 4, 1, 7, 5, 6

page 33
Answers will vary. Check to see that student additions are reasonable to fit with story.

page 34
1. I liked Ed, my elephant guide.
2. We visited the Hippo Mud Spa.
3. I took a quick dip in Lake Makat.
4. I flew over Ngorongoro Crater.

5. I camped in the fig trees near the Lerai Forest.
6. Answers will vary— something about fishing or rafting on the river.

page 35
Answers will vary. See that student expresses some purpose the author had—such as to teach something about making a mummy.

page 36
elephant—Omaha
kangaroo—Australia
porcupine—Germany
moose—Spain
lizard—Peru
8. The bear is going to Tahiti.

page 37
helicopter—Mr. Dog
sports car—Miss Cat
airplane—Aunt Frannie
motorcycle—Mr. Rabbit
bookmobile—Mrs. Bear
1. the airplane
2. the sports car
3. Mr. Dog

page 38
Answers will vary. See that student has reasonable predictions based on information in story and picture.

page 39
Answers will vary.

Answer Key

page 40

Answers will vary.

page 41

Answers will vary.

page 42

Answers will vary.

page 43

1. bored
2. excited
3. selfish
4. helpful
5. grumpy
6. frightened

page 44

Opinions
1. Hawaii is wonderful.
   I was pretty silly-looking.
   The food here is wonderful.
2. My hotel is a bit dumpy.
   I think it is also overpriced.
   The hotel staff is not friendly, and there are too many mosquitoes!
   The beach is the best part.
3. It is amazing!
   I thought the view was beautiful.

Facts
1. It lasted one hour.
   They serve meals all day.
2. It costs $100 a day because it is on the beach.
3. Today I took a helicopter tour over the volcanoes of Hawaii.

There are many active volcanoes in Hawaii.
The tour lasted 3 hours.
The helicopter pilot was from Singapore.

page 45

1. Answers will vary.
2. Great-Great-Grandpa Leonardo
3. Answers will vary.

page 46

1. . . . nose turned into icicle
   . . . fingers became ice cubes and broke off
   . . . shadow froze
   . . . drops of mist turned to snowflakes
   . . . milk came out as ice cream
   . . . words froze
   . . . stick crawled away
2. Answers will vary.

page 47

Answers will vary.

page 48

1. rowdy
2. polite or kind
3. refuse
4. not allowed
5. shrieking
6. deposit

page 49

1. insisted
2. slick
3. massive, monstrous
4. droopy, lonely

5. sticks that look like wishbones
6. ailing
7. ghostly, white

page 50

pairs of synonyms are:
destroy-ruin
weary-tired
wild-savage
prevent-stop
simple-easy
rapid-speedy
frighten-scare
steal-rob

page 51

1. a	5. c	9. b
2. b	6. a	10. b
3. a	7. b	
4. b	8. a	

page 52

1. b	4. a	7. c
2. a	5. b	8. b
3. c	6. a	9. b

page 53

1. grab
2. grand
3. reserve
4. gang
5. whole
6. more
7. country
8. take
9. stay
10. smile

page 54

hungry-eating as tired-sleeping
lawyer-courtroom as doctor-hospital
fingers-typing as feet-climbing
grumpy-happy as nervous-relaxed
monkeys-monkey as mice-mouse
cold-freezing as warm-hot

page 55

Words to circle—
   Opposites to write
bad—good
worst—best
incomplete—complete
late—early
easily—hard
none—all
sooner—later
won't—will
yesterday—tomorrow
cold—warm
midnight—noon
night—day
warm—cool
terrible—nice or good or wonderful
don't—do
less—more

page 56

Answers will vary.
   See that student has used a different and correct meaning for each word.

page 57

1. Circle all s sounds.
2. Circle beginning f sounds.
3. Circle ch sounds and t sounds in tasty truffles.
4. Circle p sounds.
5. Circle s sounds.
6. Circle c sounds.
7. Circle w sounds.
8. Circle all n sounds and the kn.
9. Circle all t sounds.
10. Circle the h sounds.